D0989818

MARJORY STONEMAN DOUGLAS:
Guardian of the Everglades

Written by
Kem Knapp Sawyer

Illustrated by
Leslie Carow

Discovery Enterprises, Ltd.
Lowell, Massachusetts
1994

© Discovery Enterprises, Ltd., Lowell, MA 1994

ISBN 1-878668-20-X hard cover / library edition; 1-878668-28-5 paperback

Library of Congress Catalog Card Number 93-72983

10   9   8   7   6   5   4   3   2   1

Printed in the United States of America

A Word on Literature

Especially recommended are the Marjory Stoneman Douglas classic, *The Everglades: River of Grass*, her autobiography, *Voice of the River*, and *Nine Florida Stories by Marjory Stoneman Douglas. Born of the Sun*, edited by Joan E. Gill and Beth R. Read, provides wonderful background material on Florida history. *The Everglades Wildguide*, by Jean Craighead George with illustrations by Betty Fraser, published by the National Park Service, is an excellent natural history resource.

Subject Reference Guide

Sawyer, Kem Knapp
Marjory Stoneman Douglas: Guardian of the Everglades
Illustrated by Leslie Carow
With a message from Marjory Stoneman Douglas
Includes Index and Map

1. Douglas, Marjory Stoneman – Juvenile Literature

2. Conservationists – Florida – Biography – Juvenile Literature

3. Everglades (Fla.) – Juvenile Literature

4. National Parks – Florida – Juvenile Literature

A Message from Marjory Stoneman Douglas

*E*very life is lived all along the way in bits and pieces that assemble into one's story. In the story are the small steps, as well as the major turns that a life takes. I have tried to live each day of my long life as a special treasure to be cherished. I have been deliberate in making the very most of every day since no day comes again except as we remember it. We cannot re-make a single day no matter how much one might wish it. Some incidents that seemed small at the time have given weight to my decisions. Together with certain larger events, they have had a significant impact on my story.

Although I have written my own autobiography, it is none-theless a remarkable experience to look back on one's life through someone else's eyes. I have just had the pleasure of hearing this biography read to me by a friend. Many people think that my life has been exemplary and worthy of interest. Of course, as I have been living it all along the way, it has its charms to me as well.

Each of your days is irreplaceable too; try not to waste them, do your best, notice life around you, make a difference to the world. When you come to the end of what should be a very fulfilling, happy experience, count the friends you have made and the lives you have touched as one measure of your own success.

Marjory Stoneman Douglas

Dedicated to Marjory Stoneman Douglas
and to friends of the Everglades everywhere

Saving the Everglades

"There are no other Everglades in the world," Marjory Stoneman Douglas once wrote. Only here can we find the Florida panther, a large and rare cat, light brown with white speckles on its shoulders and a crook in its tail. Only here can we find ancient cypress trees, some 130 feet tall and 700 years old. The trees stand knee-deep in water and provide a home for other animals—bobcats, deer, and otter. The sun shines on an alligator resting on a log near a water hole. The wood stork, a long-legged wading bird, fishes for food to bring to its young.

The saw grass, this seemingly endless river of grass, glistening in the light, blows in the wind. Each blade, with sharp edges like the teeth of a saw, grows in fresh water. The water flows along the surface of the Everglades all the way from Florida's Lake Okeechobee to the Gulf of Mexico, 100 miles south. Mounds of dry land, called hammocks, covered with live oak and gumbo limbo trees, dot the horizon. A beautifully colored snail found only in the Everglades, the liguus tree snail, attaches itself to the tree bark. The red mangrove, a tree shaped like an umbrella with roots that crowd around its trunk, appears where the fresh and salt water meet. Here the bald eagle, roosting on a limb, takes refuge.

Care for nature and all its treasures has been at the heart of Marjory Stoneman Douglas' work throughout her life. In her speaking and her writing, Marjory has shown how changes in the environment, both small and large, can threaten the entire region. The water, weather, plants, and wildlife interact in such a way that one part cannot be altered without affecting the whole. For more than half a century Marjory has warned us all that the Everglades must not be disturbed. If they are, southern Florida will suffer from a severe water shortage and many endangered animals will become extinct. The uniqueness and natural beauty of this area will be lost to future generations forever.

Marjory Stoneman Douglas has spent decades as a guardian of the Everglades. What follows is the story of her life and of the extraordinary world she sought to protect.

Northern Roots

Marjory first visited the South in 1894, when she was four years old. She travelled by train with her parents to New Orleans, then by steamship to Tampa, Florida, and on to Havana, Cuba. Her earliest memory of Florida is of someone lifting her up to pick an orange from a tree in the gardens of the Tampa Bay Hotel. The marvelous tropic sunlight was so much brighter and more inviting than the sunlight to which she was accustomed in the North.

Marjory's ancestors were the seafaring Trefethens who had come to New England from Cornwall, England. Marjory remembers hearing that "every sea in the world was known to the Trefethens." Marjory's mother, Lillian, was born in 1859 in Taunton, Massachusetts, to Daniel and Florence Trefethen. As a child, Lillian travelled to Boston to study violin with Julius Eichberg, a famous German musician. Her sister Fanny played the piano and her younger brother, Charlie, played a zither, a stringed instrument he had made himself. Later, when Charlie moved to Minneapolis to teach at the University of Minnesota, Lillian was sent along to watch over him. There she met Frank Bryant Stoneman, a Quaker by birth.

Frank was the grandson of Joshua Stoneman who had run away from his home in England to become an indentured servant in America. Indentured servants received transportation to America, as well as room and board, from their master, in return for service over a period of time, usually lasting seven years. Joshua first worked for a ship captain as a crew member. The captain then sold Joshua's indenture, or service, to a doctor in Philadelphia. After several years of service as a coachman

and medical assistant, Joshua was freed from indenture. He later moved to Virginia where he practiced medicine.

Joshua's son Mark, also a doctor, married Aletha White, a Quaker. The couple travelled west of the Ohio River with many other Quakers who wanted to settle in states where slavery was not allowed. Frank, Marjory's father, was born in a Quaker colony in Spiceland, Indiana.

One of the people in her family Marjory most admired was Aletha's aunt, Katie White. Katie and her husband, Levi Coffin, worked on the Underground Railroad to help slaves escape to freedom. They welcomed the slaves into their home in Indiana and provided a safe stopping point for many on their way north to Canada. Katie and Levi were a great source of inspiration to Marjory. She was proud of their courage and independent spirit.

After the Civil War, Mark and Aletha and their children moved farther west seeking adventure. They settled in Minneapolis where Mark practiced medicine. Exhausted by the demands of the job, he died at the age of fifty-three. After his father's death, Frank left college to help support his family. He taught school by day and, at night, cut cabbage to make sauerkraut.

A few years later, Frank, who had then become a handsome broad-shouldered young man, six feet two inches tall, left Minneapolis for Billings, Montana, to try his fortune in opening a grocery store. When the new business proved unsuccessful, Frank returned to Minneapolis. He moved into the same boardinghouse where Lillian Trefethen was living with her brother Charlie.

Frank soon fell in love with Lillian and proposed to her on a sleigh ride in a snow-covered field. The young couple returned to the Trefethen home in Taunton, Massachusetts, to be married. Lillian's parents knocked down the wall between

9

the front hall and the parlor so that Lillian could be seen as she marched downstairs for the wedding ceremony.

On their return to Minneapolis, Frank and Lillian lived in Netley Corner, the city's first apartment house. Marjory, a twelve pound baby, was born there on April 7, 1890. Her only memory of the apartment is of being fed from a pan of warm, creamed potatoes while sitting on the stairs. When Frank's building and loan business failed during the Panic of 1893, a time of widespread economic depression, the young family moved east to Providence, Rhode Island, where Frank found a job selling oil.

To Marjory, Lillian appeared to be the most beautiful woman in the world. She had marvelous black hair and eyes like brown velvet, a lovely nose, and beautiful teeth. In their new home in Providence, Lillian often gave evening violin concerts with a piano accompanist. She always began the concert by saying that her little girl was upstairs going to sleep. Then she would play the Brahms lullaby. Marjory remembers her father sitting in his big overstuffed chair and reading aloud to her from *Hiawatha*. When she first heard that Hiawatha wanted to take the bark from a birch tree to make a canoe, she burst into tears. From then on, her father skipped that section whenever he read the poem.

Frank's new business proved unsuccessful. Lillian grew bitterly disappointed and worried excessively about Frank's troubles. She dreaded the possibility of bankruptcy. When Marjory was five years old, her mother, carrying a suitcase, appeared without warning on the porch where she was playing. Lillian took Marjory by the hand and brought her to the train station. "We're going to Taunton," Lillian announced and said no more.

After the twenty mile journey, they walked into Marjory's grandparents' home on Harrison Street. No one seemed surprised to see them. Her grandparents had already eaten so Marjory and her mother ate their supper on trays in an upstairs sitting room. Marjory cried when she realized she and her mother were not just visiting. They were moving in for good.

A few days later, Lillian locked herself in her room and started to scream if anybody came near her. Marjory was told her mother was having a nervous breakdown. Lillian was sent to Butler's Sanitarium, a hospital in Providence. When she returned, her health had improved, but she was never quite the same. She seemed less energetic and clear-headed than the mother Marjory remembered.

Marjory was the only child in a house full of grown-ups. Florence, her grandmother, had a great sense of humor and loved to tell her stories—the best ones were about bears. The adults listened too, but pretended not to pay attention. An excellent seamstress, Florence made many of Marjory's clothes. Marjory had to stand still for hours while the clothes were being fitted. Her hardworking and quiet grandfather devoted himself to family, work and garden. The first in the family to awake, he spent the early morning tending the garden before joining the others for breakfast. Aunt Fanny, Lillian's younger sister, was the one who took care of everybody. She fixed breakfast and made sure Marjory got to school on time. A math whiz, she did the bookkeeping for Marjory's grandfather's brass foundry, as well as for a local bank. In her spare time she studied books about the stars and became an amateur astronomer.

Marjory grew to love the house on Harrison Street. It was a big house, three stories high, with an enormous yard, a vegetable garden, an apple tree, four pear trees, and a big cherry tree. The house had the first indoor bathroom on the street. One of Marjory's favorite places was a bedroom in the attic. Whenever she wanted to be alone, she would sneak up to the attic with her favorite doll, named Jeanne, whose dark

11

hair reminded her of her mother's. She would take a book from the bookcase which included complete sets of Charles Dickens and William Shakespeare, the Encyclopedia Britannica, histories and novels. Marjory read them all. Her family thought she should spend more time playing, but Marjory would not listen. "You couldn't drag me away from books or books away from me." Marjory once said.

The first school Marjory attended was Barnam Street Elementary, a long walk from her house. Marjory remembers that her mind was like "a dried-out sponge, ready to absorb every kind of substance there is around." She loved all her subjects except arithmetic. Her teacher once tried to explain fractions by cutting up an apple, but Marjory did not understand and consequently always hated both fractions and apples.

Marjory wrote poems and short essays which she hoped to publish in a magazine called *St. Nicholas*. Anyone whose work was accepted could be a member of the St. Nicholas League. Marjory wanted desperately to belong, but her work kept getting turned down. The magazine finally took a puzzle she invented and Marjory became a member. "It was a great moment in my life," she wrote in her autobiography.

Aunt Fanny belonged to a "bicycling club for young ladies" and often invited Marjory along on trips. For bicycling, Aunt Fanny wore a skirt that came down to the ankle, a striped shirt with a narrow starched collar, and a brown felt hat with a feather attached to it. Marjory loved the times when they bicycled around the countryside, stopping at trees to gather nuts.

Marjory studied piano at her grandmother's insistence, but she never liked practicing. "I made the most awful sounds and

mistakes on the piano and I just hated it," Marjory recalled. Whenever she hit a wrong note someone in her musical family would shout out, "That's not sharp, that's flat!" Marjory always put off practicing. Once her grandmother shouted, "When will the time come when you will practice without my telling you to?" Marjory answered, "Well, grandmother, I've never had the opportunity." Her grandmother vowed never to talk to Marjory again about the piano and Marjory stopped practicing altogether.

Marjory did agree to take lessons in public speaking, then called elocution. Unlike piano, this was something Marjory enjoyed. "I never worried about an audience—I could talk to five hundred people as well as to two people even as a child," she said.

In the winter Marjory frequently came down with colds. Whenever she had to stay home from school, she would sit in the sewing room, wrapped in a blanket near the big steam radiator. She did not seem to mind too much because she always had a good book. She looked forward to the spring when the fruit trees would be covered with different shades of pink blossoms.

On Friday afternoons, Marjory often organized a game of kick the can. She also liked to bring her friends to visit her grandfather's brass foundry. They would watch the men heat

14

the scrap metal in a big open fireplace and then pour it into a mold to cool. In another room they could see the grinding machines smooth away the ragged edges from the molded pieces of brass.

On the first of May, the children in Taunton surprised each other with May baskets filled with paper roses and candy. At twilight one child would creep up to a neighbor's porch, ring the doorbell, leave a colorful basket in front of the door, and disappear. Whoever came to the door would run out in pursuit of the one who had left the basket. Marjory believed her mother made the prettiest May baskets she had ever seen.

On summer evenings, most people in Taunton sat on their porches and watched the moonlight as it shone through the elm trees. Marjory's mother and her aunt often played the guitar and banjo and sang songs for the neighbors, who listened from their porches up and down the street. The highlight of the summer was the Fourth of July which also happened to be Uncle Charlie's birthday. He had returned from Minneapolis to Massachusetts and was living on Narragansett Bay. All the Trefethens went out to his cottage to celebrate the holiday with the first clambake of the year. They would also ride the merry-go-round and buy ice cream cones at Crescent Park.

As she grew older, Marjory became increasingly protective of her mother. "I've never been so close to anyone as I was to my mother," she once wrote. She played cards with her mother and took her on long walks. It seemed that she had become the mother and Lillian, the child. During the day, Marjory gave the impression that nothing bothered her. But, at night, nightmares frequently disturbed her sleep. She would dream that some enormous thing by her left ear was going to explode with a terrible noise. Sometimes her grandmother found her sleepwalking. Whenever she did, she would take Marjory to the window, show her the stars, and talk in a soothing voice

until Marjory started to get sleepy. Then she would lead her back to bed.

One of Marjory's friends, Margaret Blaine, took Marjory on camping trips in the summer and to dancing lessons in the winter. The Blaines' coachman drove them to class in a covered carriage, drawn by a horse named Molly. At first Marjory loved to dance, but by the time she got to high school, her attitude changed. She was scared of boys and worried that no one would ask her to dance. Marjory's mother and Aunt Fanny did not help the situation. They came to Marjory's first high school dance to check on her. Marjory was relieved to report that two boys, Fred and Herndon, had asked her to dance.

Of all Marjory's teachers the one who most inspired her was Mary Hamer, the Latin instructor. A short and heavy-set woman with sharp black eyes and black hair drawn back in a bun, she reminded Marjory of Queen Victoria. Miss Hamer believed nothing was too difficult for her students if only they wanted to learn.

Although it was unusual for a young woman to go to college in the early 1900s, Marjory had been influenced by her sixth grade teacher, Miss Dartt, a graduate of Wellesley College. This college for women, just outside Boston, had opened in 1875. Many outstanding women professors taught at Wellesley, and Marjory was pleased to be accepted as a student there. Aunt Fanny offered to pay the bills from a secret bank account where she had been saving money earned from music lessons and bookkeeping.

In September 1908, Marjory boarded the train for Wellesley. Her mother was not well enough to travel, so it was Aunt Fanny who accompanied her. She helped Marjory get settled and then left her to begin a new adventure.

Student Days at Wellesley

During her freshman year, Marjory lived in the attic of a house on Cottage Street. Her room was decorated with blue and white wallpaper and offered a beautiful view of trees from the window. The attic was without electricity so she had to study by an oil lamp. Six other girls also lived in the house. One of them, Carolyn Percy, who had a photographic memory and the ability to recite pages of trigonometry, would remain one of her best friends for life. During their sophomore year Marjory and Carolyn both moved into Fisk dormitory where they took jobs to help pay school expenses. Marjory was in charge of drying the dishes and Carolyn had to sweep the corridors, which she always did while singing at the top of her lungs.

Marjory took many courses that would influence her thinking later in life, including geography and geology taught by Elizabeth Fisher, the first woman graduate of the Massachusetts Institute of Technology. Miss Fisher had evaluated an oil field in Oklahoma and studied rocks in Russia for the czar. Marjory's social economics professor was Emily Greene Balch who would later win the Nobel Peace Prize. She led her class through the slums of Boston so they could see firsthand the housing conditions, saloons, and welfare agencies.

Malvina Bennett, Marjory's elocution professor who stressed proper articulation, repeatedly instructed her class: "Pronounce your consonants." She insisted her students recite tongue twisters in a stage whisper that could be heard from one end of the auditorium to the other. Marjory practiced saying

"Bill the boatman bumped the barge against the breastwork of the breakwater."

As a freshman, Marjory was selected for English 12, a course for composition majors. Her first assignment was to write a letter home. Marjory wrote about the beauty of the campus and was asked to read her letter aloud. The teacher criticized her "too free" writing style, but her classmates applauded. By the time she was a junior, she had her first essay published in the college literary magazine called the *Quarterly*. The following year she was made Editor-in-Chief of *Legenda*, the college yearbook.

By 1910, only a few states had granted women the right to vote. Marjory's high school Latin teacher, Miss Hamer, had

Members of the Wellesley College Equal Suffrage League, Marjory Stoneman Mary M. Rogers, and Marion A. Prinie.

often remarked that it was intolerable to think that her male students would grow up and have the vote while she did not. With Miss Hamer's words echoing in her ears, Marjory became a strong advocate of women's suffrage at Wellesley. She and five other members of the class of 1912 organized the Equal Suffrage League. This club would remain active until the nineteenth amendment to the Constitution, approved in 1920, granted American women the right to vote.

While Marjory was away at college, her mother became ill with cancer and could no longer travel. Marjory's grandmother supplied her with packs of postcards to send to her mother. Marjory managed to get a card in the mail every day for four years. She returned home for holidays and stayed by her mother's side when she had to go to the hospital for an operation.

On graduation day it was Aunt Fanny who came to watch Marjory receive her diploma. The festive occasion included parades, speeches, pageants and a tree-planting ceremony. But this joyful day ended in great sadness. After the ceremonies Aunt Fanny told Marjory that her mother's cancer had spread. Marjory returned home by train to see her mother and was able to spend a few weeks with her before she died.

Starting Out

The summer after graduation, Marjory enrolled in a department store management training program in Boston. Her friend, Carolyn Percy, had obtained a teaching job in St. Louis and suggested Marjory look for work there. In the fall Marjory followed her friend westward and found a job at Nugent's department store. She stayed in St. Louis for a year, but never felt at home living in a strange and unfamiliar city while still recovering from her mother's death. "I felt like a misfit," Marjory said, "a misfit with a job."

In 1913, Marjory moved to Newark, New Jersey, where she was put in charge of training sales clerks at Bamberger's department store. She rented a room near the store and lived by herself. In her free time, she made frequent trips to the library across the street.

One day a new friend at Bamberger's introduced Marjory to a man named Kenneth Douglas. He was a newspaper editor, tall, thin, and thirty years older than Marjory. A few weeks later, Kenneth ran into Marjory at the library and asked her out to lunch. Then he started to visit her at Bamberger's. No man had ever paid her so much attention. Three months after they first met, Marjory and Kenneth were married in a plain ceremony with only two witnesses in attendance.

But the marriage did not bring the happiness Marjory and Kenneth hoped to find in each other. After two years they realized they had little to share. Marjory made the decision to leave Kenneth. A father she had not seen in years and the possibility of a fresh start drew her south to Florida. It was a time for new opportunities.

Last Stop: Miami

Marjory, five feet one inch tall and wearing a blue taffeta dress, took an overnight train from New York to Miami in September 1915. She carried with her the few clothes she owned. Her father met her at the station. He was as tall and handsome as she remembered, but he now had a lock of gray hair that fell down over his forehead. He drove Marjory to a plain, wooden house where Lilla, Frank's new wife, came running down the steps to greet her. The warm welcome made Marjory feel at home instantly.

The Miami Marjory discovered had in large part been shaped by Henry Flagler, a businessman from Ohio who had worked for the Standard Oil Company. He had visited southern Florida in the late 1800s when the area lacked transportation and hotel facilities. Sensing opportunity, Flagler set out to develop the region as a tourist center. He started to build fancy hotels and established the first railroad along the east coast of Florida. But in 1915, the year Marjory arrived in Miami, the town was still small, its streets still covered with white sand. Fewer than five thousand people lived there. It was the kind of place where no one was terribly surprised to learn that Miss Hattie Carpenter, Miami's one high school teacher, was chased by a panther while she was bicycling home one day with a beefsteak in her basket.

Frank Stoneman had moved to Orlando, Florida in 1896, the same year Flagler had opened up the Florida East Coast Railroad to Miami. Frank studied law and then practiced as an attorney for ten years. In 1906, he took an old flatbed printing press, put it on the train, and rode south. He settled in Miami

and started the first morning newspaper, the *News Record*. He was also made a justice of the peace, and the townspeople called him "Judge."

Almost immediately, Frank became involved in a controversy surrounding the Everglades. Governor Napoleon Bonaparte Broward wanted to drain the Everglades of water so that the land could be developed for farming, housing, and business. He planned to alter the natural flow of water by building canals for drainage and transportation. Many Floridians appealed to him not to proceed until he had studied the problem thoroughly, but he would not wait. "I will be dead by that time," he answered. Frank believed the Everglades should not be drained and that the Governor must be stopped. He wrote editorials in a campaign to preserve the Everglades as they were.

Before long, Frank ran into financial difficulties in publishing the *News Record*. Threatened by bankruptcy, he sold the paper to Frank Shutts, a lawyer in town. Although the new publisher renamed it the *Miami Herald*, he retained Marjory's father as editor.

Marjory arrived in Miami with only vague recollections of her father and no idea what to expect from a stepmother. The Stonemans quickly made Marjory feel comfortable. They offered security as well as companionship. Marjory's father treated her as an equal, and she enjoyed discussing books with him. She often said that Lilla was not only her first friend in Florida, but also her best friend.

The warm climate and the sea air appealed to Marjory. She realized she was a "salt water person" and would never be happy living inland. She swam regularly early in the morning. In the evenings she often went to the beach with a group of friends and cooked by an open fire. She never learned to drive, but always found a friend willing to give her a ride.

When the society editor at the paper had to take a temporary leave to care for a sick mother, Frank asked Marjory to fill in. At first she wrote about weddings, parties, and winter visitors to the leading hotels. A clerk would come by the house on his motorcycle to pick up her copy and take it back to the office. Then Marjory began to receive assignments for more substantial news stories. She learned a lot about the newspaper business from her father. He insisted she always get the facts right and taught her to check every story for accuracy. Before long, Marjory had a regular job at the paper and was working in the office with the other three reporters.

While working at the paper, Marjory also campaigned for women's suffrage. In 1916 she and three other women, including two widows of former governors, took an overnight train to Tallahassee, the state capital, where they met with the legislators. Testifying in hearings, they urged the passage of the nineteenth amendment to the Constitution giving women the right to vote. Marjory and her companions made earnest pleas and logical arguments, but the lawmakers appeared not to listen. "It was like talking to blank walls," Marjory concluded.

This experience was Marjory's introduction to politics and her first attempt to influence lawmakers to vote for a cause dear to her heart. Her effort was unsuccessful, but she was not discouraged. Although it would take another four years, the legislature would eventually ratify the nineteenth amendment.

The First World War

World War I broke out in Europe in 1914 after the assassination of the Archduke Francis-Ferdinand, heir to the throne of Austria-Hungary, in Sarajevo, Bosnia. By 1917, Serbia, Russia, France, Belgium, England, and Japan were engaged in war against Austria-Hungary, Germany, and the Ottoman Empire. President Woodrow Wilson had tried to keep the United States out of war, but in April 1917, after Germany announced unrestricted submarine warfare and several American ships were sunk, Congress declared war on Germany.

That spring the U.S. Navy sent a ship from Key West to Miami to enlist men and women into the Naval Reserve. The *Miami Herald* had received a tip that the plumber's wife, who lived across the street from the newspaper office, was planning to be Florida's first woman to enlist. Marjory was sent to the ship to interview her. But Marjory never completed the assignment. Instead she found herself volunteering to join the Navy. When she called in to the paper, she told her father, "Look, I got the story on the first woman to enlist. It turned out to be me." He answered, "I admire your patriotism, but it leaves us a little short-handed."

The Navy put Marjory in charge of issuing boat licenses at Elser's Pier in Miami. The work offered none of the adventure that she expected. She disliked it intensely and within a year obtained an honorable discharge. Hoping to go overseas, Marjory joined the American Red Cross, an organization founded in 1881 by Clara Barton as part of an international movement to help wounded soldiers and other war victims. The Swiss had fostered this movement, and, since 1864, under the leadership of Jean-Henri Dunant, they had advocated the creation of voluntary relief agencies throughout the world. Doctors, nurses, and volunteers were not to take sides, but to remain neutral. They carried an international symbol, a flag with a red cross on a white background, to mark both themselves and their supplies.

World War I had become the bloodiest war in the history of the human race. A revolution in warfare—the first air bombings, the use of chemicals such as poison gas, and the development of armored tanks—had taken its toll on human lives. By the end of the war ten million would be dead and twenty million wounded. Countless others would die from starvation.

The task faced by all Red Cross volunteers was enormous. Marjory was assigned to a department called Civilian Relief which sent her to Europe to work with women and children refugees. She and other Red Cross volunteers sailed in a convoy of ships in September 1918. The voyage was difficult—her suitcase was stolen, the ship was blacked out to reduce the risk of attack, and the weather was rough. For several days a storm raged. After arriving in Avonmouth, England, the volunteers took the evening train to London. Here, too, the lights were extinguished as a protection against bombing. Only the dim blue lights of the underground shelters pierced the darkness.

Crossing the English Channel by boat, the Red Cross volunteers landed in the French port of Le Havre, and then boarded a train for Paris. They found a city of elegant buildings, green parks, and wide boulevards. Marjory reported to the Red Cross headquarters. She visited war refugees—mothers and children, alone, abandoned, and hungry, all in a state of shock. Many of the children were left unattended because their mothers could not care for them.

Dressed in her Red Cross uniform, a gray skirt that went down to her ankles and a heavy tunic, and armed with a free pass, Marjory travelled by train throughout France. She visited children's hospitals and clinics, and within a few weeks, was writing about conditions faced by children in the French countryside. She listened to the guns go off up and down the river in Paris on November 11, 1918, signaling the end of the war. She remembers that "they boomed out from both banks and sounded twenty to twenty-five times. All the pigeons in the Place de la Concorde rose up and flew to all the roofs. . . Thousands of people rushed into the streets. . . Everyone was kissing and shouting and crying as Paris had emptied."

Although the war was over, Marjory stayed on with the Red Cross. She continued to write reports which were distributed to American newspapers. Travelling through Europe, she saw cities which had taken centuries to build, now all in ruin.

In the fall of 1919, Marjory was sent to the Balkans (countries in southern Europe, including Montenegro, Albania, and Macedonia). She was accompanied by Captain Edwardt, a cameraman carrying a trunk full of equipment and movie film. They met many people who had no homes and others who lived in caves, desperate for food and supplies. Marjory and Captain Edwardt crossed the mountains by truck and delivered cases of powdered milk and boxes of clothing to the clinics. In Albania, finding few roads and even fewer vehicles, they climbed over mountains on horseback. Wherever they went, they visited women and children housed in Red Cross clinics.

When Marjory's work in the Balkans came to an end, she went to Greece where she boarded a steamer headed for France. Back in Paris, she discovered that the Red Cross office was closing. She did not have to hunt long for a new job. Her father sent her a cable inviting her to become assistant editor of the *Miami Herald*. She was ready to return.

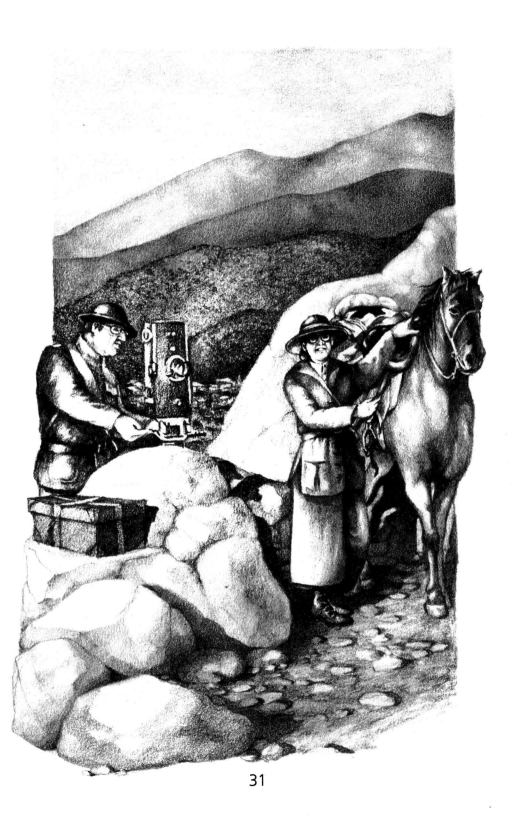

Return to Miami

The Miami which Marjory rediscovered in January 1920 had doubled in size. Hundreds of men had returned from the war to look for jobs. A greedy fever took hold as many bought land and built houses and hotels. To Marjory it seemed that what was once a little town was now exploding with reckless new building. What Marjory saw as "the delicate balance between nature and a small population" had been destroyed by "hordes of men obsessed by a manic belief in millions to be made by gambling with the prices of land for which they knew or cared nothing."

As assistant editor, Marjory was given her own column to write. She wrote about national and local affairs, often beginning each column with a few lines of verse. She earned twenty dollars a week, a salary considered decent at the time. The *Miami Herald*, unlike many other newspapers, paid men and women on an equal scale.

One of Marjory's columns, written as a ballad, was based upon the true and tragic story of a boy from North Dakota, named Martin Tabert, who had come into Florida on foot and was arrested because he was without a job or a home. Martin was thrown into a labor camp and beaten to death. The poem reads in part:

> "Martin Tabert of North Dakota is walking Florida now.
> They took him out to the convict camp, and he's walking Florida now.
> O children, the tall pines stood and heard him when he was moaning low.

The other convicts, they stood around him,
When the length of the black strap cracked and found him.
Martin Tabert of North Dakota. And he's walking Florida now.
They nailed his coffin boards together and he's walking
    Florida now."

Marjory opened people's eyes to the injustice of labor camp beatings. After the ballad was read aloud to the state legislature in Tallahassee, laws were passed to stop beatings in labor camps.

Marjory believed the newspaper should make a difference in the lives of people in the community and encouraged the *Miami Herald* to organize a Baby Milk Fund to raise money for families unable to afford milk. But when she went out into poor neighborhoods to look for families who needed milk, she began to realize that a milk fund was not enough. So much more was needed—family counselling, legal aid, job training, low-cost loans. Marjory urged her father to involve the newspaper to a greater degree, but her father was reluctant to do more. This was one of the few subjects on which Marjory and her father ever disagreed.

Writing about Florida—its geography and landscape—absorbed an increasing amount of Marjory's time and energy. She met David Fairchild, a world traveller, botanist, and collector of tropical plants who maintained beautiful gardens in Miami. Through him, she developed an interest in flowers and animals native to Florida. Several years later, the Fairchild Tropical Garden, the only tropical garden in North America, was established with the help of Marjory and others.

Marjory also met Ernest Coe, a man Marjory called "a prophet," the one who first foresaw the importance of making the Everglades a national park. A graduate of Yale University, Coe had studied landscape architecture in Europe and Japan. When he and his wife Anna first arrived in southern Florida in 1925, they discovered both a busy boom town and a strange, mysterious country called the Everglades. Although old-time residents and newcomers knew nothing of this region, Coe became fascinated by the rich plant life. He was soon spending all his time studying the Everglades and giving lectures. He became familiar with the numerous varieties of plant and animal life and tramped through the region, south to Flamingo, with its small gray houses on stilts, west to Cape Sable, and on to the dark mangrove forests of the Ten Thousand Islands. He often camped on the beach or on a pile of leaves. "The wild scream of a panther in a nearby thicket never bothered him," Marjory once wrote, and he often "fell under the spell of the million and a half wading birds."

In exploring the Everglades, Ernest Coe saw that it was the water that kept the region alive. Without the flow of fresh water, the rich diversity of plant, bird, and animal life would be absent. He believed that the only way to safeguard the Everglades was to declare the area a national park. The establishment of a national park would guarantee the preservation of the region, prevent the drainage of the water which southern Florida badly needed, and maintain a special gift of nature for the benefit of all people.

In 1872, Congress had designated Yellowstone, a vast untouched area in the west where hot springs bubble and explode and buffalo roam, to be the first national park. By 1916, there were eleven national parks, but no central organization. That same year the National Park Service was created to oversee the administration of the parks and the creation of new ones, "to conserve the scenery and the natural and historic objects and the wild life therein and to provide for the enjoyment of the same," as well as to protect them for future generations.

Coe campaigned to make the Everglades a national park every chance he got. He gave lectures to any group or club who would listen; he wrote hundreds of letters, and he travelled frequently to Washington to talk to people in government. In 1928 Coe formed the Tropical Everglades Park Association to help establish the park. Marjory joined the association, as did David Fairchild and Gilbert Grosvenor, president of the National Geographic Society. Under Coe's influence, Marjory's interest in the region grew. Over the years she worked hard to make Coe's dream come true.

A new road, called the Tamiami Trail, which would cut across the heart of the Everglades, was then under construction. It took its name from the two cities it would eventually connect—Tampa and Miami. Sometimes Marjory and a group of friends would get up before daybreak and drive along the

Tamiami Trail. They would park along the road, build a fire, cook breakfast, and watch the sun rise. Marjory loved looking out into the saw grass which covered the horizon. Everywhere she turned there were birds—the long-legged wood stork and great white heron, the roseate spoonbill with its red spoon-shaped bill, the splendid bald eagle with its white head and white tail, the snowy egret with its beautiful feathers. It was not unusual to see flights of thirty to forty thousand birds overhead.

Trips to the Everglades offered Marjory a chance to relax from the hectic pace of life at the newspaper office which, by 1924, had exhausted her. She had been under terrific pressure to produce stories and meet deadlines. Frank Shutts, the publisher, often disagreed with her and criticized her writing. Marjory worried so much that she could not sleep. Her father had hoped that she would eventually succeed him as editor, but it became more and more evident that the work was not suited to her. In 1924 Marjory's doctor convinced her to resign from the paper and rest.

Marjory says she began to recover "by being quiet, sleeping late, and by beginning to write short stories." That summer she went to Taunton to visit her grandmother and Aunt Fanny. There she wrote a short story and sent it to the *Saturday Evening Post*, then America's most well-known magazine for popular fiction. The editor, George Horace Lorimer, attracted some of the best writers of the time, including Ernest Hemingway, F. Scott Fitzgerald, and William Faulkner. He liked "At Home on the Marcel Waves," Marjory's story about a French girl who opened a beauty parlor in Miami, but wanted her to change the ending. She had to rewrite the ending two more times before he finally accepted it and gave her a check for five hundred dollars.

Marjory's grandmother could not have been more surprised when she heard the news. She had always had little faith in Marjory's becoming a writer and had wanted her to become a teacher instead. "Really, Grandmother, I think I'd rather write," Marjory once told her. "Then you will die in a garret," her grandmother said. She was convinced that as a writer Marjory would make barely enough money for food and water and would have to spend her life in a garret (an attic room). "The short story sale put everything in a different light for my family and for me," Marjory recalls. "They looked at me with new eyes."

Coconut Grove: A Place of Her Own

At the age of thirty-four, Marjory decided she was "plenty old enough to have my own house." When a friend offered to sell her a piece of land in Coconut Grove for a reasonable price, she accepted. Coconut Grove, where many artists and writers lived, was a section of Miami with beautiful tropical trees and magnificent gardens. Another friend, an architect, designed a small house on the back of an envelope. With the sketch in hand, Marjory found a contractor willing to be paid whenever money from a short story came in. Two years later the house was completed. It was so much to Marjory's liking that she once remarked, "It fits me like a glove." She furnished it simply with gifts from family and friends: a black walnut cabinet, originally used to store spools of thread, from her stepmother, and a yellow marble coffee table from her good friend, Carolyn Percy.

Marjory's house has changed little over time. It is a simple, rustic cottage made of stucco with a dark wooden frame. The house is nestled in a clump of trees and surrounded by flowering shrubs and gardenias. The main room, which serves as a living room and study, has a ceiling fourteen feet high and many windows. It is at once cozy and breezy. A large Italian desk sits in one corner, piled with books and papers. One wall is lined with bookshelves which display Marjory's large collection of books, including the Charles Dickens novels from her grandparents' house in Taunton. The main feature of her small bedroom is a special cat flap which allows her cats to go in and out as they please. A dressing room, a tiny kitchen (which for a long time contained only a hotplate and a little refrigerator) and a spare room (not much larger than a closet) for the occasional guest, complete the floorplan.

Soon after Marjory moved to Coconut Grove, she made friends with a new neighbor, Elizabeth Virrick. After learning that many African-Americans in Coconut Grove did not have running water in their apartments, Elizabeth and Marjory organized the inter-racial Coconut Grove Slum Clearance Committee. Setting up card tables outside grocery stores all over the city, they worked hard to get the necessary number of signatures to demand a vote on requiring all houses in the county to have indoor plumbing. After two years they succeeded in having water

mains and sewer lines installed. The committee also set up a fund to provide loans to residents for home improvements.

Marjory spent the first fifteen years in her new house writing short stories. Many of them were published in the *Saturday Evening Post* and others appeared in a variety of magazines, including *Ladies' Home Journal, Reader's Digest, Collier's, Woman's Home Companion*, and the *Chicago Tribune* Sunday magazine. "The Peculiar Treasure of Kings" won second prize in the O. Henry Memorial Collection of 1928. Marjory drew on her own experience as a Red Cross volunteer in Europe to write "The Story of a Homely Woman," a moving love story, which was reprinted in *Post Stories of 1937*, a collection of the magazine's best short stories published that year.

For the most part, Florida was at the heart of every tale. One of her stories, "Plumes," was based on the true story of the murder of Guy Bradley, a game warden at Cape Sable in the Everglades. By the end of the nineteenth century, hunting for birds had grown increasingly common. The birds' plumes or feathers were used to trim hats, then extremely popular items in New York shops. Because the feathers were at their finest at nesting time, the hunters would most often shoot the adult birds in their nests, forcing baby birds and unhatched eggs to be abandoned. The Florida Audubon Society, named for John James Audubon, the naturalist and painter of birds, was organized in 1901 to stop the terrible killing. That year the Florida legislature passed a law which forbade hunting certain species of birds. The Audubon Society hired Guy Bradley to protect the rookeries in Florida Bay where the birds nested. In 1905, Guy Bradley tried to stop a group of poachers from hunting snowy egrets, birds with beautiful curved feathers. One of the poachers shot Bradley and killed him. At the trial, the poacher claimed that the warden had shot first. Even though no bullets had been fired from Bradley's gun, the poacher went free.

Bradley's murder shocked the country and led to the passage of more effective national laws to protect the birds. "Plumes" aroused the interest of readers all across the country in protecting the Everglades.

GUY M. BRADLEY
1870-1905
FAITHFUL UNTO DEATH
AS GAME WARDEN OF MONROE
COUNTY HE GAVE HIS LIFE FOR
THE CAUSE TO WHICH HE WAS
PLEDGED

River of Grass

Marjory was fifty-two years old and working on a novel when she received a visit from an old friend, Hervey Allen, an author and editor of a series of books called *Rivers of America*. He wanted Marjory to write a book on the Miami River. "Hervey," Marjory said, "you can't write a book about the Miami River. It's only about an inch long." Although more than an inch long, the Miami River is a very short river running through downtown Miami. Marjory asked if she could write about the Everglades instead. "All right," Hervey agreed.

One of the first people Marjory talked to about her project was Gerry Parker, a hydrologist for the state of Florida. Gerry, who was studying the effects of water on or below the earth's surface, knew more than anyone else about the Everglades. He explained to Marjory that the Everglades were not merely swamps as many people thought, but a flow of water. "Wherever fresh water runs and the saw grass starts up, that's where you have the Everglades," he said. Marjory knew the Seminole Indians, who had lived in the area for centuries, called the Everglades "Pahayokee," which means grassy waters. She asked Gerry if he thought she could call the Everglades a "river of grass." He thought she could, and from then on the Everglades became known as the river of grass.

The Everglades was an unusual river, but a river nonetheless. It measured between fifty and seventy miles wide and an average of six inches deep. The river flowed from Lake Okeechobee, which is only fifteen feet above sea level, to the Florida Bay, dropping two to three inches a mile.

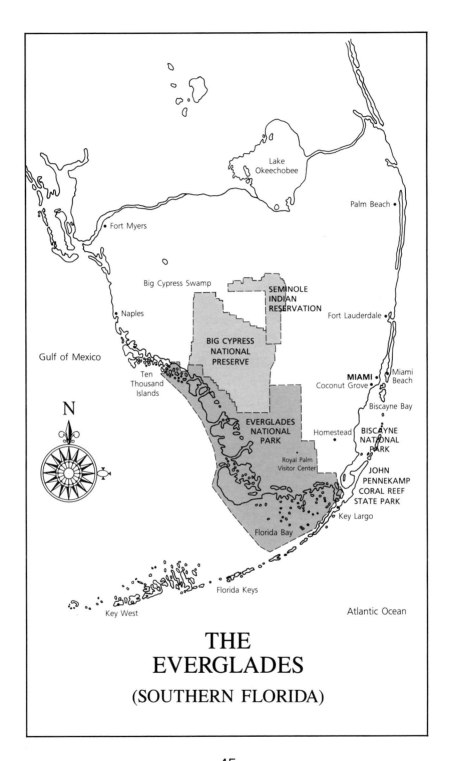

THE
EVERGLADES
(SOUTHERN FLORIDA)

"The most important contributions to this book came not from books but from the minds and memories of innumerable people who have lived in and about the Everglades for many years," Marjory wrote. "I don't know the names of half the people with whom I leaned on bridges or drank cokes in trail stations or hailed from fishing docks or gossiped with in lonely houses, on hidden roads, on beaches or by solitary rivers or on the corners of crowded streets." Two local history experts proved especially helpful to her work. Dr. John Goggin, a professor at the University of Florida and a distinguished ethnologist, who had studied the culture of Florida's Native Americans, shared his vast knowledge and helped her write the chapters on the early history of the Everglades. David True, the secretary of the Florida Historical Society and a collector of old maps, told her many stories about the Spanish settlers. A man whose hobby was searching for sunken treasure, he also talked a lot about the pirates of the Caribbean.

After five years of gathering information, talking to people, and writing, Marjory finished her book and dedicated it to her father. *Everglades: River of Grass* appeared in November 1947. Seventy-five hundred copies were printed, and in one month they were sold.

In her book Marjory describes the saw grass which has grown in the Everglades for four thousand years. With words she paints pictures of the crashing force of a hurricane in the rainy season and the windless dawn of the dry season. Through her eyes we see the variety of plant and animal life, the pine and the palmetto, the brown deer and the diamondback rattle-snake, the woodpecker and the buzzard.

Marjory also traces the history of the people of the glades —the everyday life of the Indians, the Calusa and the Tequesta, and the adventures of the European explorers. She tells the story of Ponce de Leon, the first Spaniard to explore Florida, and the Fountain of Youth he was said to be seeking. In her tales of adventures, Marjory separates fact and myth and describes both captive and conqueror.

This book gives an account of the Seminole Indian wars and the cruel attempts to remove the Native Americans from their home. The most destructive war, lasting from 1836 to 1842, led to the capture of Osceola, the "brilliant and natural leader," and resulted in the expulsion of 3,930 people, both Seminoles and African-Americans who had fought on the side of the Indian. While most were forced west into Arkansas and Oklahoma, many Native Americans were left behind "silent and unnoticed in the Everglades," Marjory writes. "They were to live and grow in numbers. They were the undefeated."

Two terrible hurricanes hit the Everglades, one in 1926, and another two years later. Marjory tells of the damage caused by the first storm: the shacks, sheds, and barns that were flattened by the wind and "trampled into mud by the machine-gunning of the steely rain." In 1928 the storm that hit Lake Okeechobee caused a flood that killed 1,800 people. Marjory writes, "Lives were smashed out under tons of water in the night, choked with mud, crushed under the weight of blown debris. . . Trains crept in slowly with supplies and coffins."

In chilling detail, Marjory explains the consequences of the efforts to drain and cultivate the Everglades. In the early twentieth century, Governor Napoleon Bonaparte Broward, headstrong and determined, wanted to build his "Empire of the Sun." To make the land suitable for housing and farming, he oversaw the building of new canals. Only later would Florida discover they had been built in vain. The drainage resulted in productive sugar cane fields and trainloads of winter vegetables —but also irreparable damage to the Everglades. The saw grass turned brown and dry; fires started and spread; ditches were dug and water pumped from canals; more crops were planted;

the soil was destroyed by overuse. The birds, snakes, small animals, alligator, and deer were threatened. Marjory calls this period "the eleventh hour," a time in which "the Everglades were dying."

Marjory asks her readers to open their eyes to the destruction and stop the excessive drainage. She ends her book with a promise of hope, "Perhaps even in this last hour, in a new

relation of usefulness and beauty, the vast, magnificent, subtle and unique region of the Everglades may not be utterly lost."

The year 1947 marked not only the publication of Marjory's book, but also the establishment of the Everglades as a national park. It had been a long battle. The United States Congress had appointed a national commission in 1929 to study the possibility of making the Everglades a national park. Among the members of the commission were Horace Albright, the director of the National Park Service, Dr. Gilbert Pearson, president of the National Association of Audubon Societies, and Roger Toll, superintendent of Yellowstone National Park.

Ernest Coe, the first to campaign for the Everglades to become a national park, and Marjory hosted an expedition through the Everglades for the commission. The party travelled by rowboat, houseboat, and blimp, a small airship that allowed its passengers the best view of the area. They saw the coral reef, tropical vegetation, sand beaches, and tangled mangrove trees. At one point they heard that a group of plume hunters had been sighted. Several members of the commission tried to persuade them to leave the birds alone. "But the night after we left to sail back to the Keys," Marjory remembers, "we heard that the hunters had shot and clubbed the adult birds to death, stripping the bloody plumes from their bodies and leaving tens of thousands of nestlings (young birds) to die of starvation or heat in the blazing sun." Marjory thought it was the death of the birds that convinced the commission to make the area a national park.

Many speculators, who had bought land and hoped to make a profit when they sold it, opposed the idea of a national park. Some people ridiculed the idea and declared the area "nothing but swamps and snakes." At one meeting, a man dumped a sackful of snakes on the table to illustrate his point. Ruth Bryan Owen, one of Marjory's good friends and the first woman from

Florida to be elected to the U.S. House of Representatives, picked up one of the snakes, hung it around her neck, and said "That's how afraid we are of snakes in the Everglades." Ruth Bryan Owen, Ernest Coe, Marjory, and others persisted and, in 1934, the United States Congress voted to establish the Everglades National Park. Opponents in the House of Representatives, however, managed to include a provision in the law that no money could be appropriated to purchase land for five years.

During World War II, people lost interest in establishing the park. When the war ended, Florida Senator Spessard Holland enlisted the help of John Pennekamp, editor of the *Miami Herald*, to lead a campaign to revive the national commission and acquire land for the park. In 1946 the state legislature provided $2 million for the purchase of private land in the area. The establishment of the park was no longer a mere dream.

Ernest Coe had hoped the park would include not only the region south of the Tamiami Trail, but also the Big Cypress area north of the trail which controlled one third of the flow of fresh water necessary for the park's survival and the water supply of southern Florida. In addition, Coe also insisted the park contain the twenty-one mile-long coral reef next to Key Largo, the only living coral reef along the Atlantic coast, with forty-one varieties of coral. Coe was adamant that the two million acres in his original proposal not be reduced. Most members of the commission, however, at a mid-winter meeting in New York to discuss the park boundaries, opposed the additional areas Coe favored. Coe, who had grown thinner with age, attended the meeting. As usual he wore his seersucker suit, now slightly worn-looking, and no overcoat. "Ernest Coe," Marjory wrote, "made his unshaken argument for the original park boundaries. If they could not be adhered to, he said, there was no use in trying to set up any Everglades National Park at all. The vote was taken. Ernest Coe's was the only 'no.' The park was assured. Coe rose and walked out into the stinging cold."

On December 6, 1947, Marjory attended the dedication of the Everglades National Park. At first Coe, still angry about the decision to limit the park boundaries, refused to attend the ceremony, but Pennekamp urged him to sit on the platform with President Harry Truman. Although Coe finally relented, he was present in body only, and not in spirit. He knew that without protection of the Big Cypress to the north, the flow of water into the Everglades could be stopped and the survival of the region endangered.

Coe did not live to see the coral reef off Key Largo become the John Pennekamp Coral Reef State Park. In 1974 the Big Cypress became a national preserve and, although oil drilling, cattle grazing and hunting were still allowed, the area became partially protected. In 1989, plans were finalized to expand the park to the east by 110,000 acres. What Coe had once envisioned, the preservation of a larger area of the Everglades, had become a reality.

Alligators, Hurricanes, and More

W hile Marjory was working on her book, she invited her Uncle Charlie, whose wife had died, to come live with her. At first, Charlie, then in his eighties, just spent the winters with Marjory, but after a few years, he stayed in her house year-round. Uncle Charlie liked to fix things. He repaired the roof and made other improvements.

Marjory and her uncle fell into a comfortable routine which they followed for more than a decade. Charlie would get up at seven, Marjory two hours later. They each fixed their

own breakfast. Uncle Charlie would go into town for his mid-day meal. Marjory made his supper—a poached egg, hot milk, toast, and tea. Uncle Charlie always retired early and then Marjory would go out with friends.

Partly because Marjory spent her days alone at home writing, she loved to go to a restaurant or a party at night. Gone were the days when Marjory dreaded attending a dance for fear of being a wallflower. She would rather go dancing than spend a quiet evening at home. Many moonlit evenings were spent swimming at the beach.

After the publication of *Everglades: River of Grass*, Marjory continued to write books. She finished the novel she had already started and called it *Road to the Sun*. She also wrote books for children, including *Freedom River*, an historical novel about three boys—the son of a Quaker abolitionist, a Miccosukee Indian, and a fugitive slave, set in Florida in 1845. *Alligator Crossing* told about alligators and illegal hunting for alligators in the Everglades. The *Key to Paris* was both a guidebook and a history of Marjory's favorite city, which had been called "the city of light," even in ancient times.

In 1958, Marjory's *Hurricane*, a thoroughly researched book filled with firsthand accounts as well as scientific infor-mation, was published. Marjory had travelled up and down the east coast, stopping at places that had been hit by hurricanes. She had visited the West Indies and talked to her cousins, Quakers from her father's side of the family, who had lived through several hurricanes. She had gone to Cuba to interview Jesuit priests who had studied hurricanes for years.

Marjory found her home in Coconut Grove the perfect place to write. "It is a fundamental truth of creative work that one has to have leisure and quiet in which to sit and think, and sometimes, just to sit, while the unconscious gathers the material," Marjory once wrote. Florida was a place where she could find "peace and quiet in which to write, even if we do have crowds of visitors." Marjory had no steady income and depended on royalties from her books to pay her bills. The neighborhood grocer let her keep an account and pay when she could. "So when I finally got around to paying him," Marjory remembers, "I wrote him a letter and I said really this book should be dedicated to Bert Albury without whose wonderful groceries this book would never have been written."

From the time she was a little girl and her father first read *Hiawatha* out loud, Marjory had always loved books. All her life she had been a faithful patron of libraries. In 1959, she founded the Friends of the University of Miami Library, an organization dedicated to supporting the library and increasing knowledge throughout the community. The group, made up of book-loving people, published a journal and held readings by local and visiting writers. One of the speakers was the poet Robert Frost, who spent his winters in south Florida.

At the age of seventy, Marjory took over the position of director of the University of Miami Press. She edited several books, including a collection of essays on the early Florida Indians by her friend, Dr. John Goggin. But the press had so little money with which to publish books that Marjory found the job frustrating and soon resigned. She wanted more time to write and to pursue a new interest, giving lectures on Florida history. Marjory started work on a history of Florida to be called *Florida: The Long Frontier.* She and a friend toured the state by car looking for out-of-the-way places and stories not yet well-known.

In her travels Marjory had made friends all over Florida. One of them, Dr. Frank Chapman, had come to Miami to study birds. He had also collected enormous research material on W.H. Hudson, the English author who loved nature. Hudson had written *Green Mansions*, the romantic story of a young man who becomes enchanted with a strange and beautiful girl in a South American rain forest. Chapman, who thought he was too old to write a biography of Hudson, had turned over to Marjory all the notes and letters gathered on his research trips. She had stored them in a drawer where they remained for several years. After the publication of the Florida history in 1967, she pulled them out and set to work.

Born in 1841, Hudson was raised on a ranch in Argentina and, as a child, grew fond of its grassy plains. He later moved to England where he wrote novels and studied birds. Marjory travelled to Argentina and England to complete her research. On one of her seven trips to England, she visited J.M. Dent, Hudson's publishing house, where she was allowed to go through a desk full of packages containing material related to Hudson.

In 1968, when Marjory was seventy-eight years old, she used an award from a Wellesley Alumnae Fellowship to make her first trip to Argentina. She met Violeta Shinya, Hudson's niece, who took her to Hudson's birthplace, seven miles outside the capital, Buenos Aires. Marjory also visited libraries and cemeteries to study the Hudson family history. She made two other trips to Argentina and brought with her portions of her manuscript for Violeta to read. On her last trip she flew to Buenos Aires and then took a small plane to Patagonia, a remote region in southern Argentina. She stayed on a sheep farm and got to know the land about which Hudson wrote *Idle Days in Patagonia.*

While Marjory was working on the Hudson biography, her eyes started to fail. "I see in a bleary sort of way," she would say. She turned to good friends for assistance with her biography of W.H. Hudson. Alice Knowles did some of the typing before she too had trouble with her eyes. Peggy Ewell, and later Clel Davis and Sharyn Richardson, also read chapters aloud and helped revise and edit the manuscript.

Friend of the Everglades

When Marjory first arrived in Miami, her father passed on to her his strong belief that the Everglades needed to be preserved. Before beginning her book on the Everglades, Marjory had written several magazine articles about the plight of birds and animals in the Everglades that would soon become extinct if serious efforts were not made to protect them. Many of the farmers in the area, however, opposed the conservationist efforts. They wanted to drain the Everglades to promote the growth of sugar cane in the rich lands below Lake Okeechobee. Cattle farmers wanted dry land for their dairy herds. Engineers, who did not understand the importance of flowing water in the Everglades, drained more and more water and built more and more canals. Soon untreated sewage and cattle manure, which had been washed into rivers flowing into Lake Okeechobee, polluted the lake and started to kill the fish.

Bird populations in the Everglades were declining. In 1870 two million wading birds were said to have populated southeast Florida. Less than a hundred years later the number had dwindled to a few hundred thousand. One species, the wood stork, had become increasingly rare because it was not able to adapt its nesting patterns to changes in the water level. The diminished number of fish on which the wood stork fed also affected the survival of the species. Life in the Everglades remained in a delicate balance. Each animal and each plant played a significant role in the web of life that made up the Everglades community. It was impossible to disturb a part without changing the whole.

Despite the creation of the national park in 1947, the Everglades were threatened by development in the areas bordering the park. In the late 1960s, an attempt was made to put an oil refinery on the shores of Biscayne Bay, the water that separates Miami and Miami Beach. This disturbed a great number of Floridians who recognized that pollution from the refinery would be tremendously harmful to the environment. The Audubon Society, devoted to the preservation of wildlife, led a successful campaign against building the refinery. But soon afterwards, developers were calling for the construction of an international jetport in the Everglades.

In 1969, Joe Browder, the head of the National Audubon Society in Miami, asked Marjory to help in fighting the jetport by making a statement to the press. Marjory said she did not think she could help his cause very much because people paid more attention to organizations than to individuals. Joe Browder was quick to respond, "Well, why don't you start an organization?" Then he took Marjory out to visit the proposed site for the jetport which was to cover thirty-nine square miles and handle sixty-five million passengers a year. It was clear to both of them that a jetport would present a danger to the environment by stopping the flow of water across the wetlands.

Marjory says she asked a friend of hers, Michael Chenoweth, "what he thought about an organization that might be called something like the Friends of the Everglades—which anybody could join for, say, a dollar." Michael handed her a dollar and said, "I think it's a great idea." With Michael's words of encouragement and a dollar bill in hand, Marjory started the organization. In a few months the number of supporters multiplied. By the end of the first year five hundred people became members of the Friends of the Everglades.

Marjory travelled all around Lake Okeechobee and through southern Florida, stopping in small towns to give a speech on protecting the Everglades. Wearing a flowery dress and a floppy straw hat, she commanded the attention of her audience wherever she went. Every time she spoke she would attract new members to the Friends of the Everglades. In two years, the Friends' membership had reached one thousand.

The Friends of the Everglades and many others worked together to prevent the jetport from being built. But even after the jetport was stopped, Marjory's organization stayed active. There was more work to be done.

One of the strongest supporters of Marjory's cause was Art Marshall, a conservationist committed to protecting the water in the Everglades. He wanted to make people understand that most of the rainfall on which South Florida depends comes from evaporation in the Everglades. As the water in the Everglades evaporates, the moisture goes up into the clouds, the clouds are blown north, and rain comes down over the Kissimmee River and Lake Okeechobee. When the lake is filled with too much water, the excess spills over into the Everglades. This again leads to evaporation and the renewal of the cycle.

Both Art Marshall and Marjory recognized the importance of preserving the water in the Everglades in order to supply water to the region. Hoping to educate the public, they showed how any attempt to drain the Everglades would endanger the community. If Florida lost the wet Everglades, it would also lose a large percent of its water.

The demand for water had increased with the growing population. When Marjory first arrived in Florida in 1915, fewer than five thousand people lived in Miami. The city population is now more than seventy times as large as it was then. This population increase has not been restricted to Miami. The entire southeastern corner of the state has grown by leaps and bounds and now numbers three and a half million. "The biggest change I have seen in Florida since 1915," Marjory observed, "is the enormous population increase. The population explosion has brought people to the state who don't know, or care, about the environment. This increase occurred upon a very fragile environment where there is a natural balance between fresh and salt water. The enormous population has completely upset that natural balance, and that is our great problem. If the people weren't here, we wouldn't have the problem with the environment—it's all a result of over-population, ignorance, stupidity and a desire of some people to make a quick buck."

Whenever she spoke, Marjory was always quick to point out the incredible waste that resulted from trying to make wet ground dry. Two thousand miles of canals costing more than seven hundred million dollars had been built. These canals had diverted the water from natural channels. Floridians had to face tearing out a section of the canals and restoring the Kissimmee River to its natural riverbed. Only then could they maintain an adequate water supply. "So many people come here thinking water comes from faucets," Marjory once said. "Somebody has to explain to them where it comes from."

Marjory wrote a plan to encourage individuals to become more involved in protecting the environment. Included were six steps:

1. Know your region.
2. Involve neighbors and friends.
3. Join a local environmental society.
4. Do what you do best to help your group.
5. Speak up. Learn to talk clearly and forcefully in public.
6. Be discouraged and disappointed at failures and the effects of ignorance, greed and bad politics—but never give up.

For over a decade Marjory wrote the *Everglades Reporter,* published by the Friends of the Everglades, and distributed to members and legislators. She spoke on radio and television and appeared before local boards, the South Florida Water Management District, the state legislature, and the Governor. She also gave lectures sponsored by the Society of Woman Geographers, an organization devoted to furthering geographical knowledge and also providing funds to help young women geographers in their work. Her book, *The Everglades: River of Grass*, has stayed in print and continues to sell ten thousand copies a year. A revised edition appeared in 1988 with a new conclusion, "Forty More Years of Crisis."

Increasingly throughout the state and the country, Marjory was recognized for her leadership role in the environmental movement to protect the Everglades. In 1975, Marjory received the "Conservationist of the Year Award" from the Florida Audubon Society. A heavy pewter plate bears the inscription, "to Marjory Stoneman Douglas, Author, Protector of the Everglades and Inspiring Leader Whose Effectiveness as a Fighter in the Cause of Conservation is Without Equal." In 1977, Wellesley College gave her the Alumnae Achievement Award. Later the Miami Wellesley Club raised money to set up an annual "Marjory Stoneman Douglas Lecture in Environmental Geography" at the college. The *Orlando Sentinel* newspaper, paying tribute to "someone who made things happen without necessarily having the tools of power on hand," chose her as the first recipient of its Floridian of the Year Award in 1983. Marjory was also the first to receive the National Parks and Conservation Association's "Marjory Stoneman Douglas Award for Citizen Conservation."

Despite the numerous honors and awards, the public's response to Marjory's stands was not always positive. Marjory was not afraid to take an unpopular position. Once, at a public hearing on the Everglades, she rose to speak and heard cries of "Go home, Granny" from the audience. Marjory, not in the least disturbed, answered, "I can't see you back there, but

61

if you're standing up, you might as well sit down. I've got all night, and I'm used to the heat.''

Marjory's eyesight had continued to deteriorate to the point of near blindness. But as she once pointed out, "No matter how poor my eyes are I can still talk. I'll talk about the Everglades at the drop of a hat.''

Marjory had also become hard of hearing. During the filming of a documentary on the Everglades, she worried that she would not hear her cue to begin talking. She suggested the crew tie a string around her ankle. When the cameraman was ready for her to speak, he would tug the string, and when he thought she should stop, he would pull the string again. The crew carried out Marjory's plan; the cameraman shot her from the waist up, and the film was a success.

Living Life to the Fullest

At the age of ninety-six, Marjory wrote in her autobiography, *Voice of the River*, "I think I enjoy old age more than I enjoyed middle age. Being let off of the responsibility of middle age is a real pleasure. Middle age is the age where everything's got to be done. Old age can be more relaxing." Throughout her life Marjory had pushed herself to work hard. Now she was willing to slow down—just a little.

In 1990, people all over Florida celebrated Marjory's one hundredth birthday. The public was invited to "bring a picnic and explore the mangroves" at the Marjory Stoneman Douglas Nature Center across the bay from Coconut Grove in a beautiful park on Key Biscayne. Festivities included a barbecue and musical presentations. When Marjory arrived in an open vintage convertible, the crowd parted for Marjory to make her grand entrance. She moved to the stage where she was seated in her Philippine chair which had been brought from her home for the occasion. After the speeches, Marjory was driven in a golf cart around the grounds. She stopped to greet the visitors, old friends, well-wishers seeking autographs, and children meeting her for the first time. Marjory had become a legend in her own time. Even at the age of one hundred, Marjory, who still had a way with words, could grab the attention of a crowd. "Eighty percent of our rainfall depends on evaporation from the Everglades. If you don't have rain and water," she would say, "South Florida will become a desert—it's as simple as that."

In Washington, Senator Bob Graham from Florida read a special birthday message to the Senate in Marjory's honor

63

and commended her for changing the way people look at the Everglades. "As we celebrate her one hundredth birthday," he said, "we remind ourselves of other lessons taught by Mrs. Douglas. That life should be lived to its fullest. That in every setback there is a silver lining. That we are the watchmen and women of all that surrounds us. It is ours to protect. And ours to preserve." He added, "We hope that each new generation will produce its own Marjory Stoneman Douglas, to devote his or her life to preserving our natural resources."

Marjory has become an inspiration to her friends and neighbors and to the world. Many of her friends believe that her greatest contribution goes even beyond her work as a writer or an environmentalist and that it lies in showing how to grow old gracefully and live life to the fullest. In her autobiography she stressed the importance of keeping up mental activity. "There's no reason you can't continue to be interested in ideas, in reading, in talking about things, in seeing what's going on," Marjory wrote. To keep informed Marjory would listen to books and news reports on tape provided by a service called "Talking Books for the Blind."

Marjory's home in Coconut Grove would change little over the years. Friends would visit daily, coming by to help with correspondence or work on the Hudson biography. Sometimes they would reminisce, but more often than not, they would talk about the present. The number of awards increased and Marjory would make room for one more plaque, bronze bird, or pewter plate. However the one award that meant the most to her is found not in her home, but rather, in the park.

The National Park Service had wanted to honor Marjory on her hundredth birthday. Marjory asked that they build a statue of a panther as a memorial not to her, but to Ernest Coe who had first dreamt of a national park. She never wanted to take credit for herself and insisted Coe be remembered for his work and perseverance in carrying through his idea. The unveiling ceremony took place on April 27, 1990 at the statue which now stands at the Royal Palm Visitor Center. The inscription includes these words, written by Marjory, "dedicated to the memory of Ernest F. Coe (1886-1951), without whose startling vision, steely endurance and indomitable will there would be no Everglades National Park today."

These words and this statue are a tribute to Ernest Coe and also to Marjory. They are a reminder of what could so easily have been lost were it not for hard work and a generous spirit.

Marjory served as president of the Friends of the Everglades and gave speeches until 1991. After that point, she no longer played as active a role in the organization, but she did stay in close touch with Joe Podgor, the executive director of the Friends. Joe has been nicknamed "Mr. Water" because of his serious concern for Florida's water supply. He speaks out for improved water quality, testifies in front of the state

legislature, and encourages volunteers to fight for the preservation and reparation of the wetlands around the world. He runs a training program to teach volunteers about environmental science, the role of government, the future of the wetlands and endangered species, problems with waste, and recycling alternatives. "The public must become the leaders," Joe says. The Friends' membership has grown to five thousand and the dues are still only one dollar—a fee Marjory has insisted the organization keep.

The Friends maintain a strong voice in support of the national park and south Florida environmental issues. They seek to arouse public interest in expanding the national park to include wetlands in the southeastern tip of the state. Another part of their mission is to reconnect Lake Okeechobee to the Everglades conservation areas through two natural water channels. These channels of water would be called the "Marjory Stoneman Douglas Twin Rivers of Grass."

In August 1992, Hurricane Andrew ripped through the Everglades, destroying hardwood trees, toppling many, pulling others up by their roots, and blowing the leaves off every branch. The storm knocked down boardwalks and platforms in the national park and damaged the visitor center and other structures. Much of the area appeared to have been hit by bombs. Florida had to deal with the potentially serious environmental problems of removing the debris. Much of the debris had to be burned. The Friends of the Everglades worked around the clock to help assess the damage and minimize air pollution caused by the burning of the fallen timber. By giving advice and support, they worked with volunteers from around the country to repair the devastation.

The preservation of the Everglades is no easy task. Marjory would want us to remember that the National Park, this river of grass, the birds, the plants, and the wildlife must be our gift to future generations. Marjory's long life will continue to inspire others to save the Everglades—to speak out and never give up hope.

Marjory was always good with words, and also quick to take action. "The Everglades must be taken care of. There's a job to do and it must be done." Her energy and commitment became her trademarks. When she walked into a room or onto a platform, people knew she could not be easily ignored. She had too much spunk.

To show their appreciation, the people of Florida have named the headquarters for the Department of Natural Resources, the state's environmental agency in Tallahassee, after Marjory Stoneman Douglas. At the dedication ceremony, Bob Graham, then governor, said Marjory "has done more than anyone else to educate the public about the Everglades." Marjory, after thanking him for his remarks, said, "But if I differ with what the Department of Natural Resources is doing, you can be sure that I will say so, whether my name is on the building or not."

About the Author

Kem Knapp Sawyer, a native New Yorker, moved to Durham, New Hampshire when she was fourteen. She is a graduate of Yale University and has taught English and drama. She and her husband Jon live in Washington, D.C. with their three daughters, Kate, Eve and Ida, and a dog named Luke. She is the author of several books for children, including *Lucretia Mott: Friend of Justice*, also published by Discovery Enterprises, Ltd. Her research for this book included visits with Marjory Stoneman Douglas at her home in Coconut Grove, Florida.

About the Illustrator

Leslie Carow grew up in Walpole, Massachusetts. After high school she headed west to Colorado State University, where she majored in landscape architecture. After graduating in 1982, Leslie studied children's book illustration and graphic design at the Massachusetts Institute College of Art and at the Manchester Institute of Arts and Sciences.

Leslie and her husband, David Ossoff, currently reside in Concord, New Hampshire, where Leslie is working as a freelance artist. Her first book for Discovery Enterprises, Ltd., *Lucretia Mott: Friend of Justice* has received outstanding reviews.

Acknowledgments

From Kem Knapp Sawyer

I would like to thank Marjory for allowing me to spend time with her and also for inspiring me. This book could not have been written without the enormous contributions of many people who shared their knowledge and memories of Marjory. Among them are Marjory's dear friends, Joan Gill Blank, Martha Hubbart, George Rosner, Nancy Brown; Joe Podgor, director of the Friends of the Everglades; Pat Tolle and Kim Middleton at the Everglades National Park; Sam Boldrick at the Miami Main Public Library; Becky Smith at the Historical Museum of Southern Florida; Jesse Kennon of Coopertown's airboat tours; Wilma Slaight of the Wellesley College Archives Office.

Special thanks as well to those who read the manuscript and gave me invaluable advice – to Jon, Kate, Eve, Ida, Kiki, Liza, and Elizabeth; to my nieces, Nikki, Carolyn and Katherine; and to the sixth graders at John Eaton Elementary School and their teacher Margaret Ellis. Kenneth M. Deitch and JoAnne B. Weisman showed great care and thoughtfulness in editing the manuscript.

I am deeply grateful to Sharyn Richardson for all her help. She is a firm believer in Marjory's work, a strong environmentalist, and a true friend of the Everglades.

From Leslie Carow

I would like to thank Kem Knapp Sawyer for her research and direction; Jeff Pollock of Discovery Enterprises, Ltd. for his technical assistance; Dawn Hug of the Historical Museum of Southern Florida; Lisa Compton from the Taunton Old Colony Historical Society; Jean Berry from the Wellesley College Archives; and Allan Strong, for providing their resources and support in this project.

A special thanks to David Ossoff and Barbara Carow for their support.

Index